Pam Wedgwood

Up-Grade!
Cello

Light relief between the grades

Spaß und Entspannung mit leichten Stücken für Violoncello Dritter Schwierigkeitsgrad
Plaisir et détente avec des pièces simples pour violoncelle Niveau 3

Cello part

FABER *ff* MUSIC

Foreword

Up-Grade! is a collection of new pieces and duets in a wide variety of styles for cellists of any age. This book is designed to be especially useful to students who have passed Grades 3 or 4 and would like a break before plunging into the syllabus for the next grade.

Whether you're looking for stimulating material to help bridge the gap between grades, or simply need a bit of light relief, I hope you'll enjoy **Up-Grade!**

Pam Wedgwood

© 2000 by Faber Music Ltd
First published in 2000 by Faber Music Ltd
Amended impression September 2003
Bloomsbury House 74–77 Great Russell Street London WC1B 3DA
Cover design by Stik
Music processed by Jackie Leigh
Printed in England by Caligraving Ltd
All rights reserved

ISBN10: 0-571-51963-6
EAN13: 978-0-571-51963-7

To buy Faber Music publications or to find out about the full range of titles available
please contact your local music retailer or Faber Music sales enquiries:

Faber Music Limited, Burnt Mill, Elizabeth Way, Harlow CM20 2HX
Tel: +44 (0)1279 82 89 82   Fax: +44 (0)1279 82 89 83
sales@fabermusic.com   fabermusic.com

1. Build that Wall

Traditional
arr. Pamela Wedgwood

2. Castaway

3. Raggle Taggle Gypsies

Traditional
arr. Pamela Wedgwood

4. Pandora's Box

Pamela Wedgwood

5. Theme from 'The Archers'

Arthur Wood
arr. Pamela Wedgwood

6. On the Level

Pamela Wedgwood

8

7. Panis Angelicus

César Franck
arr. Pamela Wedgwood

8. 2010

Pamela Wedgwood

9. Steppe on It

Pamela Wedgwood

10. Dawn Shadows

Pamela Wedgwood

11. Für Elise

Ludwig van Beethoven
arr. Pamela Wedgwood

With movement ♩ = 112

12. Humoreske

Antonín Dvořák
arr. Pamela Wedgwood

13. Journey to Egypt

1. Up the Nile

Pamela Wedgwood

2. Valley of the Kings

Pamela Wedgwood

3. Getting the Hump

Pamela Wedgwood